The Unofficial
Last of the Summer Wine Cookbook

Margaret Harker

Contents

Introduction

Last of the Summer Wine is an iconic British sitcom that ran from 1973 to 2010. It is the longest running sitcom in history.

The show is set in a Yorkshire town surrounded by beautiful hilly countryside; Last of the Summer Wine was filmed in Holmfirth and its surroundings.

The series is about a group of elderly men who engage in rather juvenile adventures. Later the show became an ensemble piece with an array of characters. The series has a lovely relaxed atmosphere and food is a part of this. The characters are often seen in a local cafe – Sid's Cafe.

Try some of the food from Last of the Summer Wine in this new cookbook.

Holmfirth

Crumpets

Ingredients

300ml/10 fl oz of milk
1 teaspoon of caster sugar
half a teaspoon of baking powder/sodium bicarbonate
200g/7 oz of white flour
half a tablespoon of dried yeast

Put the milk in a pan and warm. Put the milk in a bowl with the sugar, yeast and 70ml/2.3 fl oz of warm water. Leave for 25 minutes.

Put the flour a baking powder and sodium bicarbonate in a bowl and mix. Add the milk mix and whisk to make a batter.

Heat some oil in a pan. Put fried egg size metal rings in the pan. Put batter in the rings and cook for 6 minutes, then turn over and cook for 2 minutes.

Serve buttered

Yorkshire Pudding

Ingredients

70g/2.4 z of flour
1 egg
70ml/2.3 oz of milk
45ml/1.5 fl oz of water
vegetable oil
salt
pepper

Mix the water and milk. Put the flour in the bowl, add the egg and whisk pouring in the milk/water mix to make a batter. Add salt and pepper.

Put some oil in a baking dish. Place in a preheated oven at 218C/425F for 10 minutes until very hot. Add the batter to the pan. Cook for 30 minutes and do not open the oven during cooking.

Vegetable Soup

Ingredients

1 chopped onion
60g/2.1 oz of peas
5 chopped tomatoes
4 chopped Brussels Sprouts
half a chopped swede/rutabaga
100g/3.5 oz of chopped onion
100g/3.5 oz of chopped marrow
3 cauliflower florets
1 teaspoon of dried herbs
1 litre/2 pints of water
salt
pepper

Put some oil in a saucepan. Add the vegetables, herbs and some salt and pepper and cook for 4 minutes.

Add the water. Bring to the boil, cover and cook on a low heat for 2 hours.

Scotch Broth

Ingredients

200g/7 oz of beef chucks
200g/9 oz of chopped carrots
40g/1.4 oz of chopped swede/rutabaga
40g/1.4 oz of chopped cabbage
20g/0.7 oz of pearl barley
chopped parsley
salt
pepper

Boil the water in a saucepan. Put the pearl barley in a bowl and add the water. Leave for 5 minutes then drain and keep the water. Add the water and barley to the saucepan. Add the beef to the pan and bring to the boil. Cook on a low heat for 1 hour.

Add the swede, onions, carrots and some salt and pepper. Cook on a low heat for 2 hours. Add the cabbage and cook for 20 minutes on a moderate heat until cooked. Garnish with parsley.

Lincolnshire Sausages

There are two Summer Wine episodes where Cleggy mentions getting 'a bit of sausage for me tea'.

Ingredients

700g/1 and a half lb of minced/ground pork
half a cup of breadcrumbs
1 beaten egg
4 teaspoons of chopped fresh sage
2 teaspoons of salt
1 teaspoon of black pepper
140ml/half a cup of water
vegetable oil

Mix the ingredients. Add more breadcrumbs if needed. form into sausage shapes. Fry in oil over a medium heat for 10 minutes, turning the sausages several times.

Last of the Summer Wine Food Facts

In the episode The Waist Land, Compo has made himself a cheese and mustard sandwich. Compo's sandwiches are usually 'doorstep' ones with thick pieces of bread and huge slabs of cheese.

Holmfirth actually has a vinyard.

There is an episode where Cleggy, Compo, and Foggy have a meal of pie and peas at the pub.

Compo is clearly a man who loves his grub. He especially enjoys the puddings (both sweet and savoury) that Nora will occasionally make for him and also the sticky buns at Ivy's cafe.

The Yorkshire Post reported in 2013 that an American fan named Darin Iscrupe created a replica of Sid and Ivy's cafe at his home in Florida!

Tripe

Ingredients

450g/1 lb of sliced tripe
vegetable oil
500ml/1 pint of milk
salt
pepper

batter

200ml/7 fl oz of milk
80g/2.8 oz of flour
1 egg

Mix the batter ingredients to make a paste.

Put the tripe in a saucepan. Add the milk and some salt and pepper and cook on a low heat for 45 minutes. Drain the tripe, then dip in the batter and fry in oil until browned.

Beef Stew and Dumplings

Ingredients

400g/14 oz of stewing/chick steak chunks
1 chopped leek
1 chopped carrot
1 chopped onion
700ml/3 cups of beef stock
flour
vegetable oil
salt
pepper

dumplings

100g/3.5 oz of self raising flour
50g/1.7 oz of suet/shortening
4 tablespoon of water
salt

Mix the beef with some flour in a bowl.

Put some oil in frying pan and heat. Add the beef and cook for 5 minutes on all sides. Put them in a saucepan..

Add the leeks, onions and carrots to the frying pan. Cook for 3 minutes. Add to the pan with the beef.

Add the stock to the saucepan. Bring to the boil, then

cover and cook on a low heat for 2 hours.

Mix the dumpling ingredients to make a dough. Form into balls. Add the stew in the saucepan with some salt and pepper. Cover and cook for 20 minutes.

Last of the Summer Wine Food Facts

Roy Clarke said that, oddly, apart from him no one seemed to much like Last of the Summer Wine as a title for the show - not even the cast. However, no one could think of anything better so this title stayed in place

Sid and Ivy's cafe was more grotty and spartan at the start of the show compared to the more cosy cafe of later series.

When the show became more of an ensemble there were usually a checklist of staple scenes:

a visit to the cafe, ladies coffee session,

a visit to Wesley's shed,

Barry and Glenda having breakfast,

the captive Howard trying to work out how to get a message to Marina,

Compo bantering with Nora outside her house, and so on.

Steak and Kidney Pudding

Ingredients

380g/13 oz of chopped stewing/chuck steak
140g/5 oz of chopped kidneys
1 chopped carrot
3 chopped onions
2 tablespoons of flour
180ml/6 fl oz of stout
180ml/6 fl oz of beef stock
2 tablespoons of vegetable oil

pastry

280g/10 oz of flour
140g/5 oz of suet (or shortening)
140ml/4.7 oz of cold water

Fry the carrot and onions in half of the oil for 10 minutes. Remove from the pan.

Put the steak and kidney in a bowl with the flour and some salt and pepper and mix.

Fry the beef and kidney in the rest of the oil for 8 minutes.

Add the stout, stock and 1 tablespoon of flour to the meat. Cook on a medium heat for 8 minutes until sauce has thickened. Add the vegetables then cover and cook on a low heat for 1 hour 30 minutes. Leave to cool.

Mix the pastry ingredients to make a dough. Knead the dough for 6 minutes. Cut off about a quarter of the dough. Roll out the rest. Line a pudding basin with the dough. Add the meat mix. Roll out the other piece of dough and place on top of the bowl. Seal the top. Cover the top with parchment paper and tie the paper on.

Put a bowl upside down in a pan. Pour in boiling water so it is nearly to the level of the pan. Put the pudding on the bowl. Cover securely with a lid or tin foil. Cook on a low heat for 2 hours.

Duchess Potatoes

Ingredients

400g/14 oz of potatoes
2 tablespoons of butter
1 beaten egg
1 tablespoon of milk

Cook the potatoes in boiling water. Drain and mash to make a puree. Add the water, milk, and half the egg. Put the mix in an icing bag and pipe drops onto a greased baking tray. Brush with egg. Cook in a preheated oven at 220C/425F.

Pease Pudding

Ingredients

500g/17 oz of yellow split peas
1 chopped onion
1 chopped carrot
30g/1 oz of butter
a bay leaf
oil

Soak the peas for 12 hours in cold water.

Heat some oil in a saucepan and fry the onion and carrot for 5 minutes.

Add the peas to the pan along with the bay leaf. Cover the peas with water, cover, and cook on a low hear for 1 and half hours - until the peas are cooked.

Drain the peas - keeping some of the liquid. Blend the peas to make a paste, using some of the liquid. Season with salt and pepper and mix.

Ploughman's Lunch

Ingredients

cheddar cheese slices
crusty bread slices
cornichon pickles
apple and beetroot salad
pickle
scotch egg
butter

For salad mix chopped apple and beetroot with some lemon juice, sour cream and some salt and pepper.

Butter the bread, Serve with side dishes.

Scotch Egg

Ingredients

200g/7 oz of pork mince
200g/7 oz of sausage meat
6 eggs
3 tablespoons of chopped sage and parsley
40g/1.4 oz of flour
100g/3.5 oz of breadcrumbs
1 tablespoon of English mustard
milk
oil

Put four of the eggs in a pan with some water and bring to the boil. Simmer for 5 minutes. Put the eggs in some cold water for 10 minutes, then take the eggs out of the water.

Mix the meat with the mustard and herbs.

Peel the eggs.

Put some clingfilm on a board. Put some of the meat on the clingfilm and roll the meat out so it is enough to cover an egg. Make four meat patties.

Roll the eggs in flour. Put each egg in a meat patty. Press the meat around the egg to make a ball like shape with the egg inside the meat.

Dip each ball into some flour, then some beaten egg and the breadcrumbs.

Fry the balls in hot oil for about 6 minutes - until golden.

Toad In The Hole

Ingredients

6 pork sausages
1 egg
70ml/2.4 fl oz of milk
50ml/1.7 fl oz of water
70g/2.4 oz of flour
oil
salt
black pepper

Cook the sausages under a hot grill for 6 minutes on each side.

Put the flour in a bowl along with some salt and pepper. Add the egg, milk and water whisking all the time to make a batter.

Put some oil in a baking tin. Place in a preheated oven at 220C/430F for 8 minutes. Put the sausages in the tin, then pour over the batter. Put the tin back in the oven and cook for 35 minutes.

Scotch Egg

Steak and Kidney Pudding

Meat and Potato Pie

Ingredients

450g/1lb of beef cut into cubes
2 boiled potatoes cut into cubes
1 chopped onion
shortcrust pastry
salt
pepper

Put the beef, onions and some salt and pepper in a pan containing 550ml/1 pint of water. Cook on a low heat until the beef is cooked.

Drain the contents of the pan and keep the liquid.

Put the beef, onion and potatoes in a pie dish. Add some of the reserved liquid. Cover with shortcrust pastry.

Cook in a preheated oven at 200C/400F for 45 minutes.

Last of the Summer Wine Facts

In the series 7 episode The Waist Land Foggy has a money making scheme selling junk food to residents of a health farm!

In one episode Cleggy has a jar of beetroot he can't get open. Foggy declares he will open it - which naturally results in a comical disaster for Foggy.

Compo clearly has a sweet tooth because he puts a huge amount of sugar in his tea.

Compo often pours some tea from his cup into his saucer and drinks it. This habit was developed in the 19th century in numerous countries. By pouring some of the tea in the saucer it can be cooled before drinking.

Drinking tea from saucers became popular among working class people at work as they would only have a short time for a tea break and could not drink very hot tea in the short time.

Sausage Roll

Ingredients

sausage meat
puff pastry
black pepper
dried thyme
dried sage
egg

Mix the sausage meat with the pepper, thyme and sage.

Roll out the puff pastry. Cut into two long rectangles. Put the sausage meat down the centre of the rectangle shaped pastry. Brush one side of the pastry beside the sausage meat with beaten egg. Fold the pastry over the sausage meat. Seal down the edge. Cut the pastry into sausage shape pieces.

Put the sausage rolls on a baking tray. Bake for 20 minutes in a preheated oven at 200C/400F until the meat is cooked and the pastry is golden.

Apple Sauce

Ingredients

450g/1 lb of apples peeled, cored and sliced
2 teaspoons of butter
two and a half teaspoons of sugar
two tablespoons of water

Put the apples in a saucepan with the water. Boil for 5 minutes - until they have softened. Mix in the sugar and butter.

Rub the apple mix through a sieve. Heat up the sauce before serving. Serve with pork or other white meats.

Serve with meats such as poultry or pork.

Mint Sauce

Ingredients

mint leaves
3 tablespoons of white wine vinegar
5 tablespoons of hot water
1 tablespoon of caster sugar
salt

Sprinkle some salt on the mint and finely chop. Put in a jug with the sugar and boiling water, mix, and leave to cool down. Add the vinegar and stir.

Traditionally served with roast lamb in England.

Stuffed Marrow

Ingredients

1 deseeded marrow cut into half with the seeds removed
1 chopped onion
1 chopped clove of garlic
40g/1.4 oz of peas
4 tablespoons of sweetcorn
2 finely chopped mushrooms
1 chopped and deseeded pepper
170g/6 oz of grated cheddar cheese
2 teaspoons of chopped herbs e.g. rosemary, thyme
oil

Fry the onion in some oil for 7 minutes. Add the garlic and pepper and cook for another 5 minutes. add the peas, sweetcorn and most of the cheese and mix.

Put the marrow pieces in a roasting tray. Put the mix in the marrow pieces. Put some cheese on top.

Cook at 180C/350F for 40 minutes.

Cauliflower Cheese

Ingredients

1 cauliflower, cut into florets
45g/1.5 oz of butter
45g/1.5 oz of flour
400ml/14 fl oz of milk
100g/3.5 oz of grated mature cheddar cheese
salt
black pepper

Put the cauliflower in a saucepan of salted water. Bring the water to the boil and cook for 4 minutes - taking care not to overcook. Drain the cauliflower.

Put the butter in a saucepan. Heat to melt the butter, then stir in the flour to make a paste. Remove the pan from the heat and stir in the milk. Cook on a medium heat and bring to the boil. Then cook on a low heat for two minutes.

Remove from the heat, then stir in two thirds of the cheese, and some salt and pepper. Put the cauliflower in a baking dish. Pour over the cheese sauce, and sprinkle the rest of the cheese on top.

Cook in a preheated oven at 190C/375F for 30 minutes - until the top has browned.

Mushy Peas

The episode Spring Fever indicates that Compo is a fan of mushy peas.

Ingredients

400g/14 oz of frozen peas
2 teaspoons of chopped mint
1 teaspoon of butter
salt
black pepper

Put the peas in a pan of boiling water and cook for 4 minutes until cooked. Drain. Put in a bowl with the butter, mint and some salt and pepper. Gently mash with a fork or a potato masher.

Fish Cakes

Ingredients

250g/9 oz of fish such as salmon, haddock, cod with the skin and bones removed
2 peeled and chopped potatoes
1 chopped onion
1 egg yolk
1 egg
1 tablespoon of chopped parsley
1 tablespoon of lemon juice
50g/2 oz of flour
breadcrumbs from 2 slices of brown bread
olive oil
butter
oil
salt
black pepper

Put the fish in some tin foil with a drop of olive oil. Cook in preheated oven at 200C/400F for 14 minutes - until the fish is cooked. Chop the fish into pieces.

Make the potatoes into mash, ad mash them with some butter.

Cook the onion and garlic in some butter for 5 minutes. Put in a bowl and add the potato, fish, egg yolk, lemon juice and parsley. Mix.

Make 10 cakes from the mix. Dip the cakes in flour with a little black pepper in it, then dip them into some beaten egg, then in the breadcrumbs.

Put some oil and some butter in a pan and cook the fishcakes on a medium heat for 10 minutes - cooking on both sides until browned.

Meat Patties

Ingredients

230g/8.11 oz of cooked chopped beef
1 chopped onion
30g/1.5 oz of suet (shortening or lard can be used)
60g/3 oz of flour
3 tablespoons of gravy/stock
salt
pepper

Mix the ingredients. Make into 8 balls.

Put on a baking tray and cook in a preheated oven at
200C/400F.

Bubble and Squeak

Ingredients

cooked mashed potato
cooked cabbage
butter
salt
black pepper

Use equal amounts of potato and cabbage.

Chop up the cabbage. Add to the potato and some salt and pepper. Mix well.

Melt some butter in a hot pan, then add the potato mixture to the pan and smooth down into a pancake like shape. Fry until one side is cooked, turn the Bubble and Squeak over and turn the other side.

Liver and Bacon

Ingredients

500g/18 oz of lamb's liver
7 slices of bacon
1 chopped onion
a beef stock cube
chopped sage
500ml/1 pint of water
half a tablespoon of flour
salt
pepper

Put the onion and bacon in pan and fry on a medium heat until browned.

Add the water, liver, flour beef stock cube some sage and some salt and pepper to the pan. Stir, and cook on a low heat for 40 minutes.

Hotpot

Ingredients

4 pork chops
2 sliced kidneys
2 sliced onions
3 sliced apples
650g/1.4 lb of sliced potatoes
240ml/1 cup of stock
chopped sage
salt
pepper

Put a layer of potatoes and onion in a baking dish. Add some sage and salt and pepper. Add a layer of pork chops, kidneys, apple, potato, onion and some sage, salt and pepper. Top with a layer of potatoes.

Pour the stock over the top.

Cook in a preheated oven at 140C/275F for 3 hours.

Last of the Summer Wine Food Facts

Cleggy is sometimes seen eating toast when he is at home. There is usually marmalade too.

Sid's Cafe in Holmfirth, which you can visit now in real life, offers a menu of sandwiches and toasted sandwiches, homemade soup, toast, and jacket potatoes. They also serve scones, teacakes, and fruitcake. It is generally traditional English cafe grub.

Cleggy, Compo, and Foggy rarely buy anything other than a cup of tea in Ivy's cafe - which would partly explain why Ivy finds them irritating. They don't do much for Ivy's profits.

Sometimes they will have a cake such as a sticky bun.

On occasion they have some cooked food - which is usually something like egg or sausage and chips with beans.

Ivy is never pleased when anything is left on the plate!

One of Mike Grady's big breaks was doing Pepsi commercials. Mike played a nerdy sort of character in the commercials.

Fish and Chips

There is a fish and chip shop in Holmfirth named after Compo. Compo's is located at 9 Burnlee Rd, Holmfirth. The reviews are very good and there are lovely surroundings outside to eat

Ingredients

4 haddock or cod fillets
6 potatoes peeled and cut into thick chip/fry shaped pieces
220g/8 oz of self raising flour
300ml/10 fl 0zs cold lager beer
vegetable oil
salt
black pepper

Wash the potatoes in cold water. Dry with a cloth, then out them in a pan of hot oil for 8 minutes. Remove the chips from the heat and place on a plate to cool.

Coat the fish in some flour and salt and pepper. Whisk the flour, lager and a pinch of salt in a bowl together to make a batter. Dip the fish in the batter then put the fish in a pan of hot oil and cook for 10 minutes - until brown. Remove from the heat and place on a plate.

Put the chips in the hot oil and cook for 3 minutes until crisp. Drain the chips and serve with the fish.

Mushy Peas

Chocolate Eclair

Jam Tarts

Ingredients

85g/3 oz margarine
170g/6 oz of self raising flour
strawberry jam

Mix the margarine and the flour together - using a little water if needed - and make a dough.

Roll out the dough. Cut out circular shapes - about 15cm in diameter.

Put the dough shapes into a baking tray for cupcakes/muffins and put some jam on top. Put the tray in preheated oven at 200C/400F for 25 minutes - until the pastry is browned.

Bread Pudding

Ingredients

250g/8.8 oz of dried or stale bread
60g/2.11 oz of suet
30g/1 oz of sugar
2 tablespoons of marmalade
60g/2.11 oz of dried fruit
1 egg
milk
ground ginger

Put the bread in a bowl. Add some water and leave for 12 minutes. Squeeze the bread. To drain the water. Add the ingredients and mix. Put the mix in a greased cake tin. Cook in a preheated oven at 190C/374F for 1 hour.

Rhubarb Crumble

Ingredients

650g/22 oz of chopped and trimmed rhubarb
2 tablespoons of caster (superfine) or golden caster sugar
3 tablespoons of lemon juice
1 teaspoon of butter

for crumble topping

240g/8 and a half oz of butter cut into pieces
400g/7 oz of flour
200g/7 oz of caster sugar/golden caster sugar

For the crumble, place all the ingredients in a bowl and mix, rubbing the ingredients together.

Put the rhubarb in a greased (with butter) baking dish. Put the sugar on the rhubarb along with the lemon juice and butter. Spread the crumble topping on top of the rhubarb. Sprinkle some sugar on top,

Cook in a preheated oven at 180C/350F for 13 minutes - until the top has browned.

Serve with custard or cream.

Jam Roly-Poly

Ingredients

75g/2 and a half oz of suet
130f of raspberry jam
175g of self raising flour
2 tablespoons of caster sugar
120ml/4 fl oz of milk
15g/half an oz of butter
salt
custard

Put the flour and butter in a bowl. Add the butter using fingertips. Add the suet and sugar. Mix. Add the milk, then use a knife to make a dough.

Roll out on a floured board/surface. Make a rectangle, about 8 and a half inches x 11.8 inches/22cm x 30cm.

Cover the dough with jam, leaving a small dough border round the edges. From the shorted end, roll up the dough. Pinch together the edges and twist the ends.

Wrap the dough in foil, leaving some extra room for the dough in the foil.

Take a roasting tin and put a wire rack in it. Put a piece of greased baking paper on it. Put the dough in the foil in the wire rack. Add hot water to the baking dish - make sure it does not touch the foil.

Cook in a preheated oven at 200C/180C for 45 minutes.

Serve with custard.

Last of the Summer Wine Food Facts

We see Cleggy buying some apples in one episode.

Foggy has been known to put customers off their food in Ivy's cafe with his tales of things he had to eat in the jungle!

Louis Emerick who plays P.C. Walsh came third in the 2008 series of BBC cookery competition Celebrity Master Chef.

Barry Wilkinson is often seen enjoying a boiled egg for his breakfast before he departs for the building society.

Roy Clarke said that Last of the Summer was never meant to be realistic or about the past. The show takes place in a rather idyllic make believe world where everyone knows each other and life is a bit slower and more whimsical than the real world.

The initial plan was for Last of the Summer Wine to be set in the Yorkshire town of Rotherham. In the end though they decided that town was a little bit too urban for the show they had in mind.

Rock Cakes

Ingredients

130g/4.5 oz of dried fruit
110g/3.8g of butter
2 teaspoons of allspice
1 teaspoon of dry ginger powder
1 beaten egg
85g/3 oz of sugar
3 tablespoons of milk
220g/7.7 oz of flour
1 teaspoon of baking powder

Mix the baking powder, flour ginger and allspice in a bowl. Add the butter and mix - to make a breadcrumb type mixture.

Add the fruit and sugar and Mix. Add the egg and milk. Make a dough. Make 10 pieces from the dough. Bake in a preheated oven at 180C/356F for 25 minutes.

Brandy Snap

Cream Slice

Rhubarb Fool

Ingredients

700g/1.5 lb of rhubarb
custard
cut into pieces
40g/1.4 oz of caster sugar
1 teaspoon of allspice

Put the rhubarb and sugar in a pan. Cover and cook on a low heat for 20 minutes.

Drain the rhubarb. Mix with the custard and allspice. Put into individual glasses and refrigerate for 1 hour before serving.

Toffee

Last of the Summer Wine merchandise has included clotted cream Last of the Summer Wine toffees.

Ingredients

200g/7 oz of caster sugar
100g/3.5 oz of brown sugar
170g/6 oz of golden syrup
200ml/6.7 fl oz of cream
160ml/two thirds of a cup of condensed milk
130g/4.5 oz of butter
2 tablespoons of vanilla extract

Mix the brown and caster sugar, golden syrup, condensed milk, butter and cream in a pan. Cook on a moderate heat until the temperature reaches around 125C/257F. Remove from the heat.

Add the vanilla extract. Put into a greased cake tin. Leave to cool. Cut into pieces.

Custard Creams

Ingredients

220g/7 oz of butter
100g/3.5 oz of custard powder/vanilla pudding mix
220g/7.7 oz of flour
100g/3.5 oz of caster sugar
2 tablespoons of milk
1 tablespoon of vanilla extract

cream filling

1 tablespoon of custard powder/vanilla pudding mix
260g/9 oz of icing sugar
130g/4.9 oz of butter
1 teaspoon of vanilla extract

For the biscuit/cookie dough, mix butter, sugar, milk and vanilla extract to make a paste. Add the floor and custard powder ans make a dough. Put the dough in the refrigerator for 30 minutes.

Slice the dough into small square cookie/biscuit shapes. Put on a baking tray on baking paper and cook in a preheated oven at 180C/356F for 10 minutes.

Mix the filling ingredients to make a paste. Spread the filling on a biscuit. Put another biscuit on top. Repeat with all the biscuits and filling.

Spotted Dick

Ingredients

260g/9 oz of self raising flour
130g/4.5 oz of suet
190g/6.7 oz of currants
90g/3.1 oz of caster sugar
1 tablespoon of lemon zest
160ml/2 thirds of a cup of milk

Mix the flour, suet, zest and sugar.

Add the milk and make a dough.

Shape the dough into a rectangle shape. Wrap in parchment paper and tie with string. Put in a steamer over a pan of boiling water. Cover. Steam for 1 hour 40 minutes over a low heat.

Serve with custard.

Apple Tarts

Compo is very fond of apple tart and custard. We know this because he requests it from Nora - just prior to getting a bucket of water over his head!

Ingredients

chopped cooking/green apple
grated Wensleydale or cheddar cheese
150g/5.2 oz of flour
85g/3 oz of lard or butter
a pinch of salt
2 tablespoons of milk
honey
beaten egg

Mix the flour, lard, salt and milk and make a dough.

Roll the dough into 16 circle shapes. Put half in buttered tart tins.

Add chopped apple, honey and grated cheese in each tart and cover with pastry. Put the pastry tops on each tart and seal. Put a small hole in each tart and glaze with beaten egg.

Cook in a preheated oven at 230C/450F for 30 minutes - until browned.

Trifle

Ingredients

sponge cake pieces
2 chopped bananas
almonds
3 tablespoons of strawberry jam
300ml/1 and a quarter cups of thick cream
500g/1.1 lb of custard
100ml/3.3 fl oz of orange juice

Put the sponge in the bottom of a glass bowl. Add the orange juice. Add the raspberry jam and then the bananas. Pour over the custard then add the cream. Top with almonds.

Refrigerate for a few hours before serving.

Fruit Cake

Ingredients

500g/1.1 lb of dried fruit
100g/3.5 oz of mixed/candied peel
80g/2.8 oz of almonds
3 eggs
160g/110 lb of butter
160g/110 lb of sugar
180g/6.3 oz of flour
1 tablespoon of orange zest
100ml/3.3 fl oz of orange juice
apricot jam

Mix the orange juice, orange jest and dried fruit. Leave for 12 hours.

Mix the butter and sugar to make a paste. Add the eggs and whisk them in. Add the flour and almonds. Add the fruit, peel and almonds. Put the mix in a cake tin lined with parchment paper. Cook in a preheated oven at 170C/338F for 1 hour, then 150C/302F for 2 hours.

When it is cooled brush apricot jam on top.

Last of the Summer Wine Food Facts

At the Summer Wine gift shop in Holmfirth you can buy clotted cream fudge and shortbread in a Last of the Summer Wine themed box.

When the show began in 1973, the price board in Ivy's cafe lists fish & chips as costing 25p!

Peter Sallis narrated a commercial for Polo mints in 1994. Polo mints without holes.

Brian Wilde did an advert for Clover butter spread in 1985. Not as Foggy obviously!

The White Horse in Holmfirth was used a lot when the characters go to the pub. You can visit this pub in real life and there are mementos and photographs from the show on display.

Sid and Ivy's cafe has Beale printed on it some early episodes. It is never confirmed though whether this is their name.

Mint Humbugs

Ingredients

400g/14 oz of brown sugar
140ml/4.7 fl oz of water
3 drops of peppermint extract

Put the sugar and water in a pan. Cook on a low heat for 10 minutes - until sugar has dissolved. Bring to the boil - to about 148C/ 300F and cook until the water has gone.

Add peppermint. Put mix on a plate. Cut into pieces and leave to harden.

Chocolate Eclair

In the ladies 'coffee morning' scenes there is always a battle over who will get the chocolate eclair or cream cake. The losers have to make do with a biscuit.

Ingredients

melted chocolate
3 beaten eggs
50g/1.7 oz of flour
45g/1.5 oz of butter cut into pieces
1 teaspoon of sugar
whipped cream
130ml/4.3 fl oz of cold water

Mix the water and butter. Mix the flour and sugar.

Put the water and butter mix in a saucepan. Boil then take off the heat. Add the flour and sugar mix and make a smooth paste using a whisk or electric whisk. Beat in the eggs.

Pipe the mix onto a greased baking sheet - making finger shapes.

Bake in a preheated oven at 200C/400F for 120 minutes. leave to cool. Top with melted chocolate. Leave to cool.

Put a hole in the end of each eclair. Pipe in whipped

cream.

Blancmange

Ingredients

8 sheets of gelatine
35g/1.3 oz of cornflour
1 litre/5 cups of milk
2 tablespoons of lemon zest
280g/9 oz of caster sugar

Put the gelatine in cold water.

Put the cornflour in a pan with 5 tablespoons of milk. Add the rest of the milk and the sugar and lemon zest. Bring to the boil. Then cook n a low heat stirring all the time for 10 minutes. Drain the gelatine and add to the milk. Cool, remove zest then put in a jelly mould, Place in the refrigerator for 12 hours.

Crumpet

Spotted Dick

Victoria Sponge

Nora Batty is sometimes critical of the sponge cakes made by other women in Last of the Summer Wine. Nora clearly prides herself on making a good sponge cake.

Ingredients

100g/3.5 oz of butter
100g/3.5 oz of caster sugar
2 eggs
100g of flour(self raising)
strawberry jam
icing sugar

for filling

120g/4.2 oz of butter
210g/7.4 oz of icing sugar
60ml/2.2 fl oz of cream

For the filling, mix the ingredients together to make a paste.

Mix the butter and the sugar to make a paste. Add the beaten egg. gradually whisking the mix. Fold the flour into the mix. Put the mix into two greased cake tins. Cook in a preheated oven at 170C/325F for 30 minutes. Leave to cool.

Put filling, then the jam on top of one cake. Put the other cake on top. dust with icing sugar.

Treacle Tart

Ingredients

pastry

113g/4 oz of flour
30g/1 oz of butter/margarine
salt
water

filling

100g/3.5 oz of breadcrumbs
6 tablespoons of golden syrup
1 tablespoon of treacle

milk

Mix the pastry ingredients to make a dough. Leave for 30 minutes. Roll out the dough and place in a greaseproof flan dish.

Mix the syrup and treacle. Add the breadcrumbs. Add the mix to the pastry case. Brush the edges with milk.

Cook in a preheated oven at 190C/475F for 30 minutes.

Jam Tarts

Ingredients

85g/3 oz margarine
170g/6 oz of self raising flour
strawberry jam

Mix the margarine and the flour together to make a dough.

Roll out the dough. Cut out circular shapes - about the size of muffins.

Put the dough shapes into a baking tray for cupcakes/muffins. Put some jam in them. Put the tray in preheated oven at 200C/400F for 30 minutes.

Sticky Toffee Pudding

Ingredients

200g/7 oz of flour (self raising)
2 eggs
165g/5.8 oz of brown sugar
80g/2.8 oz of butter
1 teaspoon of baking powder
2 tablespoons of treacle
250ml/8.4 fl oz of milk

sauce

80g/2.8 oz of butter
1 tablespoon of treacle
100g/3.5 oz of brown sugar
200ml/6.7 fl oz of cream

Mix the treacle, eggs, baking powder, sugar and flour in a bowl. Mix well. Add the milk, stirring continuously to make a smooth batter. Place in greased baking dish. Cook in a preheated oven at 180C/356F for 40 minutes.

For the sauce: mix the butter, treacle, brown sugar and cream in a pan. Simmer for 10 minutes. Bring to the boil. Pour over the toffee pudding.

Tea Cakes

Ingredients

300g/10 oz of dried fruit
90g/3.17 oz of chopped glace cherries
90g/3.17 oz of brown sugar
450ml1 pint of black tea
2 beaten eggs
1 teaspoon of mixed spice/pudding spice
270g/9.5 oz of self raising flour

Mix the glace cherries, eggs, allspice and sugar. Add the flour and mix to make a batter.

Line two rectangular cake tins with buttered grease proof paper and add the mix. Cook in a preheated oven at 150C/302F for 1 and a half hours.

Rice Pudding

Compo makes reference to Nora's cold rice puddings in Last of the Summer Wine.

Ingredients

110g/3.8 oz of rice (pudding or long grain)
4 teaspoons of caster sugar
butter
600ml/2 and a half cups of milk
a teaspoon of nutmeg

Grease a baking dish with butter. Add the milk, rice, nutmeg and sugar. Mix.

Cook in a preheated oven at 160C/320F for 1 hour 50 minutes.

Brandy Snaps

There is an episode where Cleggy and Truly enjoy some brandy snaps. Brandy snaps are a popular snack or dessert food similar to the Italian cannoli.

Ingredients

113g/4 oz of treacle
56g/2 oz of margarine
113g/4 oz of flour
113g/4 oz of sugar
half a teaspoon of ginger

Heat the treacle and the margarine together. Then add the flour, sugar and ginger and mix well.

Place teaspoonfuls of the mixture on a hot baking sheet and cook in hot oven for 5 minutes. Roll the snaps around a wooden spoon handle when still hot.

Fill with cream.

Cream Slice

In the episode Magic And The Morris Minor Auntie Wainwright was ordered by her Doctor to not be so mean with money so she bought the most expensive cake from Ivy's Cafe - a cream slice.

Ingredients

25g/1 oz of dark chocolate
450g/1 lb of puff pastry
3 egg yolks
45g/1.5 oz of caster/superfine sugar sugar
3 tablespoons of flour
3 tablespoons of cornflour/starch
140ml/4.7 fl oz of double cream
240ml/1 cup of milk
120g/4.2 oz of icing/confectioners' sugar
1 vanilla pod

Roll out the pastry and cut into a thin 32x22cm/13 inches x 9 inches piece. Put a piece of pastry on a baking sheet lined with greaseproof paper. Put another piece of greaseproof paper on top. Cook in a preheated oven at 200C/392F for 20 minutes. Cool then cut into three rectangular pieces.

Put the milk in a pan and almost bring to the boil.

Mix the egg yolks, caster sugar and a few tablespoons of the warm milk in a bowl. Add the plain and cornflour and mix in the rest of the milk.

Put the mix in the pan and bring to the boil stirring all the time to make a thick batter. Add the vanilla pod and leave to cool. When cold whisk until a smooth mix is made. Add the double cream and whisk to make a thick mixture. Put the mix in a piping bag.

Mix the icing sugar with a 3 tablespoons of water to make the frosting.

Pipe the half the mix on one of the pastry pieces. Put another on top and pipe the rest of the mix on. Put the last pastry piece on top. Put the frosting on top. Drizzle melted chocolate on top. Refrigerate for 30 minutes then cut into slices.

Curd Tart

Ingredients

60g/2.11 oz of currants
230g/8.11 oz of curd cheese
230g/8.11 oz of shortcrust pastry
90g/3.17 oz of butter
2 egg yolks
2 egg whites
pinch of nutmeg
lemon peel

Whisk the egg yolk until a stiff paste is formed.

Roll the shortcrust pastry out, cut into circles and line individual tart tins with it.

Mix the butter, egg yolks, sugar and curd cheese. Add some lemon peel, the dried and nutmeg. Gently mix in the egg white.

Put the mix in the tart cases and cook in a preheated oven at 180C/350F for 35 minutes.

Tea Cakes

Ingredients

300g/10 oz of dried fruit
90g/3.17 oz of chopped glace cherries
90g/3.17 oz of brown sugar
450ml/1 pint of black tea
2 beaten eggs
1 teaspoon of mixed spice/pudding spice
270g/9.5 oz of self raising flour

Mix the glace cherries, eggs, allspice and sugar. Add the flour and mix to make a batter.

Line two rectangular cake tins with buttered greaseproof paper and add the mix. Cook in a preheated oven at 150C/302F for 1 and a half hours.

Photo Credits

Cover

https://commons.wikimedia.org/wiki/File:Stonewalls_and_rocky_fields_around_Todmorden_and_Hebden_bridge.jpg

Alesia Ofori

13 April 2019

Cream Slice

https://commons.wikimedia.org/wiki/File:Mille-feuille_20100916.jpg

Georges Seguin

16 September 2010

Steak and Kidney Pudding

https://commons.wikimedia.org/wiki/File:London-Meal_in_a_pub.jpg

Ji-Elle

11 January 2023

Chocolate Eclair

https://commons.wikimedia.org/wiki/File:Eclairs_with_chocolate_icing_at_Cafe_Blue_Hills.jpg

georgie_grd

12 January 2008

Crumpet

https://commons.wikimedia.org/wiki/File:Buttered_crumpet.jpg

LoopZilla

27th April 2005

Scotch Egg

https://commons.wikimedia.org/wiki/File:One_scotch_egg_(No_jar_of_Marmite).jpg

Unhindered by Talent

2012

Brandy Snap

https://commons.wikimedia.org/wiki/File:Brandy_snap.jpg

Pauline Mak

12 March 2011

Mushy Peas

https://commons.wikimedia.org/wiki/File:Vegan_fish_and_chips_with_mushy_peas.jpg

Mx. Granger

4 July 2021

Spotted Dick

https://commons.wikimedia.org/wiki/File:King_of_Spotted_Dicks.jpg

plambertuk

18 June 2012